SPECIAL
★OPS II★

Marine Scout Snipers in Action

by Jessica Rudolph

Consultant: Fred Pushies
U.S. Special Operations Forces Adviser

BEARPORT
PUBLISHING

New York, New York

Credits

Cover and Title Page, © Lance Cpl. Tommy Bellegarde, U.S. Marine Corps; 4, © AFP/Getty Images; 5, © Cpl. Stephen M. Kwietniak; 6, 6B, © Laurent Rebours/Associated Press; 7, © Anja Niedringhaus/Associated Press; 8, © Rob Curtis/AFP/Newscom; 9, © Cpl. Michael Petersheim; 10, © Lance Cpl. Joseph Scanlan; 11, © Lance Cpl. Maxton G. Musselman; 12, © Aflosports/Newscom; 13, © Spc. Hillary Rustine; 14 © Department of Defense/ Department of the Navy/U.S. Marine Corps; 15, © NARA/PD-USGOV; 16, © Associated Press; 17, © Sgt. James Harbour; 18, © Craig Allen/Getty Images; 19, © Presselect/Alamy; 20, © U.S. Air Force Photo/Alamy; 21, © Rob Curtis/AFP/Newscom; 22, © Shilo Watts/Getty Images; 23, © Stocktrek Images; 24, © Scott Olson/Getty Images; 25, © Laurent Rebours/ Associated Press; 26TL, © R. Carner/Shutterstock; 26–27, © U.S. Marine Corps photo by Staff Sgt. Ezekiel R. Kitandwe/Released; 28TL, © Lance Cpl. Maxton G. Musselman; 28TR, © U.S. Marine Corps; 28–29, © U.S. Marine Corps photo by Lance Cpl. Kyle J. Keathley/ Released; 29T, © Photo courtesy of Eberlestock.

Publisher: Kenn Goin
Senior Editor: Joyce Tavolacci
Creative Director: Spencer Brinker
Design: Debrah Kaiser
Photo Researcher: We Research Pictures, LLC

Library of Congress Cataloging-in-Publication Data

Rudolph, Jessica.
  Marine scout snipers in action / by Jessica Rudolph ; consultant, Fred Pushies, U.S. SOF adviser.
      p. cm. — (Special ops II)
  Includes bibliographical references and index.
  ISBN 978-1-61772-891-4 (library binding) — ISBN 1-61772-891-8 (library binding)
  1. Snipers—United States—Juvenile literature. 2. United States. Marine Corps—Commando troops—Juvenile literature. I. Pushies, Fred J., 1952– II. Title.
  UD333.R83 2014
  359.9'84—dc23
                                        2013005973

For more information, write to Bearport Publishing Company, Inc., 45 West 21st Street, Suite 3B, New York, New York 10010. Printed in the United States of America.

10 9 8 7 6 5 4 3 2 1

Contents

An Attack in Basra

Gunnery Sergeant Jack Coughlin's heart was pounding.
It was March 2003. Jack's **convoy** had been winding through
a street in Basra, Iraq, when a hidden gunman opened fire.
Bullets flew toward the Marines—but where was the shooter?
It was Jack's duty as a Marine Scout Sniper to find out.

Basra is the second-largest
city in Iraq, after Baghdad.

Jack grabbed his rifle. He jumped out of the **Humvee** he was riding in and crouched behind it. Jack peered through the gun's **scope**, scanning the rooftop of a nearby building. He saw nothing. Then Jack noticed the shadow of a man behind a bush. There was the shooter.

Humvees are large military vehicles used to move troops and carry supplies.

Jack Coughlin was part of the first group of American forces that invaded Iraq in 2003. The troops were sent to take down Iraq's **dictator**, Saddam Hussein.

Jack Coughlin

Stopping the Ambush

The shooter whom Jack spotted was an Iraqi army soldier. From behind the bush, he kept firing at the convoy. Bullets struck the American trucks and tanks. Jack had to hurry. Marines' lives were at stake. He had to stop the enemy gunman at once.

Jack (left) aiming his rifle

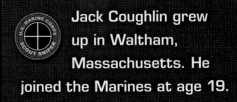

Jack Coughlin grew up in Waltham, Massachusetts. He joined the Marines at age 19.

The shooter was about 1,000 yards (914 meters) away—about the length of ten football fields. Jack pulled out his rifle and adjusted his aim. He took a slow, deep breath, then firmly pulled the trigger. The bullet hit the Iraqi soldier, causing him to fall backward. Jack's bravery and quick action that day stopped the **ambush**, saving the lives of countless Marines.

Marines on patrol in Iraq

Scout Snipers

Marine Scout Snipers like Jack have an important job. They help stop enemies from harming U.S. troops and innocent **civilians**. How? Snipers are trained to shoot at dangerous **targets** from distant hidden locations. They also track down enemies to gain information about them. This is known as **reconnaissance**. Reconnaissance helps U.S. soldiers prepare to fight the enemy.

A sniper's rifle has a scope on the top that makes objects appear larger.

Scout Snipers often work in teams. One man is the scout, or spotter, and the other works as the shooter. Scouts use special equipment, such as **binoculars**, to observe the enemy and to tell the shooter where to aim his rifle. The shooter's job is then to fire his gun at the target without being seen.

This is what a sniper sees when he looks through a rifle scope.

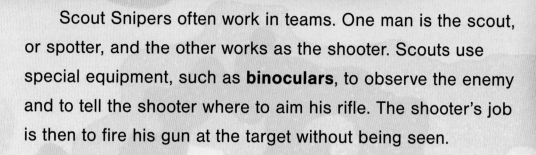

The lines inside a sniper's rifle scope are called crosshairs. Snipers try to hold their rifles steady enough so the target they're aiming at appears where the lines cross, making an X.

Shooters' School

Who has what it takes to become a Scout Sniper? Only Marines in top shape are considered for Scout Sniper training. To get into a Scout Sniper school, Marines must pass a physical fitness test and an intelligence test. They must also be excellent shooters.

To be considered for sniper school, a Marine must be very strong and able to lift heavy equipment.

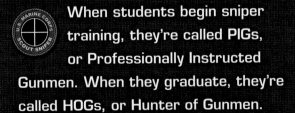

When students begin sniper training, they're called PIGs, or Professionally Instructed Gunmen. When they graduate, they're called HOGs, or Hunter of Gunmen.

After being accepted into a training program, students are taught how to become even better shooters. They learn how to measure distance and wind speed. Why? A strong wind can affect the path of a bullet, blowing it off course. After weeks of practice, students take a shooting test in which they fire at steel targets up to 1,000 yards (914 meters) away! Some of the targets are moving, just like enemies on a battlefield. To pass this test, students need to hit 80 percent of the targets.

Sniper school students shooting at steel targets

Learning to Disappear

Marine Scout Sniper students also learn how to **stalk** enemies. Snipers need to know how to track their targets without being seen or heard. Students also take classes on **camouflage**. They learn how to make their own **ghillie suits** out of fabric, plants, and other materials. These suits help them blend into their surroundings and creep up on enemy targets.

A ghillie suit can save a Marine from being spotted by the enemy.

The stalking test is even more difficult than the shooting test. Students have four hours to sneak within 200 yards (183 meters) of an instructor in an outdoor course. The course is located within a field that has long grass, trees, and other hiding places. The sound of grass rustling or leaves crunching can easily give away a student's position. If the instructor sees or hears the student before he reaches the 200-yard (183 meter) mark, he fails.

Graduates of Scout Sniper school are given a bullet to wear around their necks called a HOG's tooth. It's a kind of good-luck charm meant to protect them in battle.

These men have graduated from the nine-week Marine Scout Sniper training course. About 30 percent of students fail to graduate.

Invisible Enemies

The Marine Corps first opened Scout Sniper training
schools in the 1940s, during World War II (1939–1945).
Marines learned a lot from these schools, but they also learned
from enemies in battle. When Americans invaded islands in the
Pacific Ocean during World War II, they found a hidden enemy
aiming right at them.

**Marines storm the shore of the
Pacific island of Saipan while hidden
Japanese snipers shoot at them.**

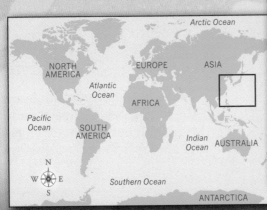

Japanese snipers quietly waited in the jungle for the American soldiers to walk by. They painted their faces green and wore ghillie suits made out of leaves, branches, and coconut plants. The Japanese soldiers blended perfectly into the islands' thick grasses and tall palm trees. Through their encounters with Japanese soldiers, the Americans learned how to use camouflage to become almost invisible.

Japanese snipers learned how to copy bird and animal calls. They used these sounds to cover up the sounds of their movements and to distract their enemy.

The jungle environment that some soldiers fought in during World War II was completely new to most American troops, but Marine snipers quickly learned how to hide, just like their enemy.

Wanted Dead or Alive

In the 1960s and 1970s, the U.S. Military fought against another enemy that hid in the jungles. This time soldiers were fighting in the Vietnam War (1954–1975). One of the most skilled fighters in Vietnam was Marine Scout Sniper Carlos Hathcock.

U.S. Marines in Vietnam

Carlos was very good at stalking and targeting the enemy, the **Viet Cong**, in the dense forests of Southeast Asia. After the Viet Cong realized how many soldiers they had lost to Carlos's rifle, they put a **bounty** on his head. The Viet Cong often paid people $8 for each American sniper they could capture. For Carlos and his partner, though, the bounty was $30,000! Thanks to Carlos's skills, no one ever collected that bounty.

Carlos (center) is considered a legend among Marines. After his service in Vietnam, he went on to train other Marine Scout Snipers.

Carlos Hathcock died in 1999 from a disease called multiple sclerosis. After his death, the military named a shooting range in California in his honor.

New Challenges

Marine snipers have faced different challenges in recent wars. After **terrorists** attacked the United States in 2001, American troops invaded Afghanistan. Two years later, in a separate war, the United States invaded the nearby country of Iraq. Since that time, American forces have rooted out terrorists and **insurgents** in both countries.

On September 11, 2001, terrorists hijacked several planes and crashed them into buildings in New York City (below) and Virginia. One of the planes crashed into a field in Pennsylvania.

In Afghanistan and Iraq, Scout Snipers have faced extremely dangerous situations. They are forced to fight in busy cities filled with civilians and on steep, **rugged** mountains. Also, the enemies in these places use different **tactics** than in previous wars. For example, terrorists try to confuse U.S. forces by not wearing uniforms, making it hard for Marines to identify the enemy. However, snipers have learned how best to target terrorists—and, ultimately, save lives.

Marines patrolling the streets of a busy city in Iraq

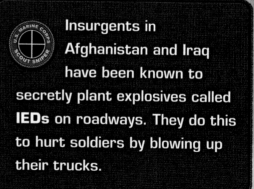

Insurgents in Afghanistan and Iraq have been known to secretly plant explosives called **IEDs** on roadways. They do this to hurt soldiers by blowing up their trucks.

Man Versus Machine

In Iraq and Afghanistan, the U.S. military is using new aircraft called **drones** to attack enemies. However, snipers continue to prove their worth. They are often better than machines at carrying out certain missions.

Drones are aircraft controlled by pilots on the ground. Many fire missiles or drop bombs. Others take photos of people, vehicles, and buildings on the ground.

For example, snipers can spot important details that drones cannot. They can tell if a person looks nervous and might be hiding a weapon. Although drones take good-quality pictures of vehicles and people, they cannot capture this kind of information. Drones are also more likely to harm innocent civilians when they fire a missile in an attack. Snipers and their guns are much more precise than missiles and seldom hit civilians.

A drone in flight

Marine Scout Snipers are some of the most accurate shooters in the world.

Driving Away Enemies

Marine Sergeant Jonathan Charles discovered how valuable Scout Snipers are when his unit arrived in southern Afghanistan in 2010. Every time Marines stepped off the American **base,** insurgents fired at them. As a result, several Scout Sniper teams were sent to the area to help protect the Marines.

The mountains of southern Afghanistan

The camouflaged snipers hid between boulders and in mud homes. They patiently waited for insurgents to appear. When one did, they took aim. Within a few months, 185 insurgents were killed by unseen Marine Scout Snipers. Word of the deadly snipers spread and the attacks on the base stopped. "They quit altogether," Jonathan said.

This sniper peers over a mud wall in Afghanistan.

With the enemy under control, Jonathan Charles's unit could focus on their main goal—training Afghan soldiers and protecting civilians.

Knowing When Not to Shoot

One of the hardest challenges Scout Snipers face is knowing when *not* to shoot. In 2003, Jack Coughlin was perched on a roof in Afak, Iraq. His job was to protect the Marines **patrolling** the streets below. Suddenly, he noticed a suspicious man on a street corner, not far from the Marines.

When the battlefield is in a city, there are possible threats to Marines from enemies hiding on rooftops and in windows and doorways.

Jack placed his finger on his rifle's trigger and watched. Several cars pulled up next to the man and then sped away. Then Jack saw something that looked like the end of a gun in the man's pocket. Jack was ready to fire. Was the man an enemy or a civilian? Suddenly, the man reached into his pocket and pulled out—a cell phone. Relieved, Jack put down his gun.

Jack Coughlin (left) greets local Iraqis.

Bullets travel faster than the speed of sound. Therefore, a sniper's bullet may hit the enemy before he or she hears the shot fired from the gun.

Lives Saved

In 2005, Jack retired from the Marines. He received a Bronze Star medal for his heroic actions in the Iraq War. The sergeant is proud of what he and his fellow Marines accomplished and all the lives they saved.

Bronze Star

In 2010, there were about 300 snipers in the Marine Corps.

Although Jack hated taking human lives, he knows he had one of the most important jobs in the military—protecting American troops and civilians from enemy threats. "It is much better to think of lives saved than human beings killed," says Jack.

A Marine Scout Sniper platoon in Iraq

Marine Scout Snipers' Gear

Marine Scout Snipers use lots of equipment to carry out their missions. Here is some of the gear they use.

In a Scout Sniper team, spotters use equipment such as **high-powered scopes** and **binoculars** to find targets.

Night-vision goggles allow Scout Snipers to see targets at night by magnifying small amounts of light. When soldiers look through the goggles, everything they see appears green.

Scout Snipers usually carry a standard sniper rifle such as an M40A3 or this **M107SASR**.

Scout Snipers carry their gear—including ghillie suits, radios, and digital cameras—in **backpacks** that can weigh up to 100 pounds (45 kg).

Glossary

ambush (AM-bush) an attack from a hidden position

base (BAYSS) the place where soldiers live or operate from

binoculars (buh-NAHK-yuh-lurz) tools for seeing a close-up view of things that are far away

bounty (BOUN-tee) a reward offered for the capture of a person

camouflage (KAM-uh-flahzh) a covering or coloring that makes people blend into their surroundings

civilians (si-VIL-yuhnz) people who are not in the military

convoy (KAHN-voy) a group of military vehicles traveling together for safety

dictator (DIK-tay-tur) a person who has complete control over a country and usually runs it unfairly

drones (DROHNZ) airplanes without pilots that are flown by remote control

ghillie suits (GIL-ee SOOTS) camouflage clothing designed to look like plants

gunnery sergeant (GUN-ur-ee SAR-juhnt) a rank in the Marines above staff sergeant

Humvee (hum-VEE) a jeep-like military vehicle that can move troops and supplies over rough roads

IEDs (eye-ee-DEEZ) letters that stand for improvised explosive devices; homemade bombs, often set off by remote control

insurgents (in-SUR-jints) people who fight against a lawful government or lawful leaders

patrolling (puh-TROHL-ing) watching or walking around an area to protect it

reconnaissance (rih-KAHN-uh-zinss) the gathering of information about an enemy

rugged (RUHG-id) rough; jagged

scope (SKOHP) a type of telescope used to find faraway targets; sometimes mounted on top of a rifle

stalk (STAWK) to track someone in a quiet, secret way

tactics (TAK-tiks) ways of doing things to win a battle

targets (TAR-gits) things or people that a shooter aims at

terrorists (TER-ur-ists) individuals or groups that use violence and terror to get what they want

Viet Cong (VEE-iht KAWNG) an army supported by North Vietnam that fought against the United States and South Vietnam governments during the Vietnam War (1954–1975)

Bibliography

Afong, Milo S. *HOGs in the Shadows: Combat Stories from Marine Snipers in Iraq.* New York: Berkley Caliber (2007).

Coughlin, Gunnery Sgt. Jack, Capt. Casey Kuhlman, and Donald A. Davis. *Shooter: The Autobiography of the Top-Ranked Marine Sniper.* New York: St. Martin's Press (2005).

Senich, Peter R. *U.S. Marine Corps Scout-Sniper: World War II and Korea.* Boulder, CO: Paladin Press (1993).

The official Web site of the U.S. Marine Corps:
www.marines.com

Read More

David, Jack. *United States Marine Corps.* Minneapolis, MN: Bellwether Media (2008).

Lunis, Natalie. *The Takedown of Osama bin Laden (Special Ops).* New York: Bearport (2012).

Sandler, Michael. *Today's Marine Heroes (Acts of Courage).* New York: Bearport (2012).

Souter, Gerry, and Janet Souter. *War in Afghanistan and Iraq.* London: Carlton Books (2011).

Learn More Online

To learn more about Marine Scout Snipers, visit
www.bearportpublishing.com/SpecialOpsII

Index

About the Author

Jessica Rudolph lives in California.
She has edited and written many children's books
about history, literature, science, and nature.